PAUL BARKSHIRE'S

UNEXPLORED LONDON

Lennard Publishing
1 9 8 7

Lennard Publishing
a division of Lennard Books Ltd
The Old School, Brewhouse Hill
Wheathampstead, Herts
AL4 8AN

British Library Cataloguing in Publication Data

Barkshire, Paul
Paul Barkshire's unexplored London
1. Photography – Landscapes 2. London
(England) – Description – 1981 – Views
I. Title
779'.99421085'0924   TR660.5

ISBN 1 85291 005 4

Designed by Pocknell & Co
Printed and bound in Great Britain by
Butler & Tanner Ltd,
Frome and London
Photoset in Garamond Original by Jigsaw Graphics

Thanks to all who have made this
book possible including my publishers, David Bailey, the London boroughs
who have bought my prints, especially Victoria Library, Guildhall Library,
Camden Libraries and the National Monuments Record.
Also thanks to The Photographers' Gallery,
family and friends who have helped during difficult times,
and the owners of the interiors I've photographed.

P D BARKSHIRE

CONTENTS

FOREWORD

Paul Barkshire is a man obsessed with the truth. His eyes cannot lie, distort or dramatise. This is not his choice, it is just his nature. Paul is a modern day Johnny Appleseed, travelling around, planting a visual image on his 8×10 negative in the same innocent way.

I see him in the romantic light of a craftsman, who through this craft transcends the normal, in the same way that Weegee went beyond the press picture and Lartigue beyond the snap. How to explain this magic? I can only give examples like those mentioned above, or add a few like Rousseau or, dare it be said, Beaton.

The sophistication of Paul's images is their simplicity, so much so that they are rather chic in the best meaning of the word.

To consider Paul's work, two other names will be mentioned: Edwin Smith, and the great French photographer Atget, but I believe Paul has very little in common with these two sentimental greats. There is nothing Proustian about Mr. Barkshire. I find him closer to nineteenth-century French architectural photographers, such as Balthus.

Paul Barkshire the man, is the personification of his work. If I were casting him, he would clearly get the part. He may over-play the role a bit, with little idiosyncracies like making a point of not signing prints, but after all it is the images that count, and here they count very highly. His photographs are perhaps the most important documentation we have seen of England.

Paul is unique. He is honest; the kind of honesty that started a long time ago with some cave paintings in France. If I compare him with this unknown cave man who just had to paint what he saw because he could not do it any other way, we won't be far from Paul.

DAVID BAILEY

INTRODUCTION

I was born in London, in Greenwich Hospital on 24 March 1953. My parents were living in nearby New Cross at the time, and soon after my brother was born in November 1955, we moved out of London to Slough. It was on a school trip to London in, I think, 1963 that I took my first photographs, but I do not remember it as the beginning of a lifelong interest. In the summer of that year we moved further away, to Markfield near Leicester, where we lived for three years. Then on 31 May 1966 we emigrated to Montreal, Canada.

One Christmas, 1969 or 1970, I was given an instamatic camera but was disappointed with the quality of the pictures, and soon lost interest. At that time I was more interested in taking LSD than taking pictures. A few years later, I started using the instamatic again and took lots of snapshots until it broke. I then bought a good 35mm SLR and a set of lenses, although at this time I was taking pictures rather than *making* pictures. I certainly didn't pay much attention to the results.

The next year, 1975, my attitude changed. I spent the summer in England, staying with my Mum and sister who now lived in Windsor, and I found that I enjoyed visiting and photographing historic places and buildings. When I returned to Canada in September, I bought darkroom equipment and printed my black and white pictures. I found that printing my own pictures made me concentrate more on the results and I put more thought into taking pictures after that. I also became interested in the history and art of photography.

By 1976 I was obsessed with photography and though I didn't think I would do commercial work, I knew I wanted a job that had something to do with photography. In September I started working in a photo lab, processing film, printing black and white prints and posters. In October I started a course in commercial and portrait photography at The School of Modern Photography in Montreal. The course was taught on one night a week for about twenty weeks, and we worked with 4×5 inch view cameras which were new to me.

I liked the quality of the 4×5 inch contact prints so much I wanted my own view camera. Then when I saw some 8×10 inch transparencies at the School, I decided that an 8×10 camera would be best for contact prints and began to look for a second hand camera. The owner of a camera shop in Lachine, where I lived then, said he had an 8×10 somewhere in the basement and would look for it when he had time. I went to the shop often until one day, at the end of March, the camera was there. What a disappointment. It looked like it had just been found on a rubbish dump. It was dirty, the bellows were dried out and in such bad condition that they would have to be replaced, the ground glass was smashed and there were bits of glass in the frame and bellows. But I couldn't find an 8×10 anywhere else so I bought it for $75.

By the end of June 1978 the camera, an Eastman View No 2 of around 1925, was ready, with new bellows custom made in Rochester, a 375mm Ilex lens, and an old Majestic tripod. I cleaned the brass and wood of the camera, but the spring back seemed weak compared with the backs of the 4×5s at the School of Modern Photography: Would it work?

To find out, I set up the camera in the back yard. It was marvellous to see a brightly lit scene on the ground-glass. I took one picture and processed the negative right away. It was fogged on one side. I couldn't believe it after all the money I'd spent. I set up the camera again in the back yard and took another picture. This time I held my arm diagonally across the back, and pressed in the back when I withdrew the dark-slide. After taking the picture I pressed in the back and put the dark-slide back in the film holder. I went straight to the darkroom and processed the negative. It was good, not a trace of fog, and I couldn't wait to make and print pictures from the 8×10 negatives.

During July and August I took some pictures in Montreal with the 8×10. I liked the results but I didn't want to photograph Montreal. I wanted to photograph historic places and so I decided to move back to England, as I thought I might be able to earn a living from photography. I thought there *must* be a market for sharp, grainless, contact prints of historic buildings, and although my 8×10 pictures were not very good, I knew they would improve as I got used to the camera. I admired historic and modern photographers who photographed the urban scene; Marville, Atget, Abbott, Tice and Friedlander. That's what I wanted to do. I thought I would give it a try for three years.

So I moved back to England at the end of September 1978. I was able to live in Windsor with my Mum and sister for three years, so my cost of living was not high. In October I bought a 240mm Symmar lens, second hand, as the 375mm lens had too narrow a view for many of the pictures I wanted to take. As I didn't have much money I had to sell my 35mm camera and lenses. Since then I've used no other format but 8×10.

At the end of October I took my first good pictures with the 8×10 and at the end of November I photographed West Wycombe for the National Trust. I thought I was off to a good start, but by the beginning of April 1979 I'd spent more than I'd earned. During the first half of 1979 I spent all my time taking photographs in and around Windsor, London, and West Wycombe Park for the National Trust.

I wasn't doing any commercial work, and my only income was from a few print sales and the work for the National Trust. I needed more money, so I wrote to the City of London Guildhall Library, with a sample print, asking if they would buy prints that I took of the City. They replied that they would be interested in any work I did in the City, so during the last half of 1979 I photographed old buildings, passages and courtyards in the City.

At this time I didn't know print sales to libraries would be my main income, so I was selling prints at cost price. In the winter of 1979-1980 I taught photography at Windsor College to supplement my income and to allow me to continue photographing buildings. In February I sold prints taken in Westminster to the City of Westminster Local History Library and they said they would buy most of the pictures I took of Westminster. I managed to get a slightly better price per print and decided to concentrate on photographing London.

I made this decision not just because the Guildhall and other libraries were interested in the work. I could see that central London was changing rapidly, especially the City and that much would soon be gone, and I wanted to photograph as much as possible before it was too late. The more I photographed London, the more devoted I became to making a portrait of it.

In May 1980 I put the price of prints sold to libraries up, and that year I started selling prints to other London borough libraries; Richmond, Southwark, Camden and Islington. I also photographed Stourhead, Bradenham, Cliveden, Blaise Hamlet and Powis Castle for the National Trust.

At the beginning of 1981 it was now obvious sales to libraries was my main income and would be for some time. They were still very cheap, the costs of using 8×10 being high, but some libraries were buying many prints and couldn't afford very much. I did more work for the National Trust, but I still wasn't earning enough money so I worked as a labourer during the winter of 1981-82.

Despite that slight extra income, at the beginning of 1982 things looked very bleak. My three years were up and I wasn't earning a living from photography. My Mum had moved to a smaller house in Windsor and I no longer had a bedroom. I was sleeping on the dining room floor, and felt under pressure to get a real job and move out. But the crisis just made me more determined to succeed in what I wanted to do.

By now I'd built a collection of over 1600 prints but to make a living from print sales to libraries I needed to sell two sets of prints. I wrote to The National Monuments Record, and they said they would like to buy prints but could not afford to pay very much. Although I was disappointed with the price, in May I started sending them prints in batches of 30. The extra money helped.

In the summer I showed some prints to the Photographers Gallery in London, to let them know what I was doing, and I was surprised at the interest they took in the work. On one of my photographic trips to Mayfair I met David Bailey

and Terence Donovan and was invited to David Bailey's to show prints. I met Martin Harrison at Bailey's and they bought 21 prints. This gave a great boost to my confidence at a time I was often thinking of giving up.

In November I moved to South East London and gradually things improved to the point where I never thought of giving up full time photography. In January 1983 the Victoria and Albert Museum bought some of my work and in March the Photographers Gallery asked for 10 prints for the exhibition Contemporary European Photographers, touring Italian towns. With The National Monuments Record buying work from me at the standard price for libraries, I could just about earn a living from print sales to libraries.

At the beginning of

1984 I was given two exhibitions, at Fingerprints Gallery in Muswell Hill and at the Photographers Gallery, both in London. Since then my prints have been sold from the print room of the Photographers Gallery. My work for libraries continued, so that I now have over 6,000 prints in various public collections.

My method of photographing London has been basically the same since 1978. I'll first read about the area I intend to visit, then check every building mentioned, photograph them if the conditions are right, and explore the area and photograph interesting or old buildings not mentioned in books. It's not usually possible to photograph everything I want in one visit, so I return time and time again and take

more. There are some buildings in London that always fascinate me — these I photograph many times.

Although I photograph many subjects of relevance to local history libraries, for the last few years I've concentrated on a particular subject each year, as well as the various other subjects. In 1985 I concentrated on historic interiors and in 1986 shop and pub interiors. In 1987, I have been photographing modern buildings.

When I've exposed 10 or more negatives I process the film in trays, 2-4 negatives at a time. My favourite film is Tri-X Pan but because this film wasn't available here in 8×10 until 1984 I've used Plus-X, Ilford Ortho, FP4, HP4 and HP5. Tri-X Pan is now the film I use most though I also carry a few sheets of Tri-X Ortho,

Gravure Positive and Vericolor II type L.

I print on fibre papers, archivally processed, and toned with selenium. I've used many papers but my standard papers have been Ilfobrom, then Pal Print, and now Oriental Seagull. After processing, the prints are air dried on blotters and then flattened in a dry-mount press. The negatives are numbered and captioned with India ink and this shows in the black border of the prints.

Until 1983 I worked with just the two lenses mentioned. I bought a 300mm lens in that year and 155mm lens in 1985. That year I also bought a new 8×10 camera, a Wista Field DX, to replace the old Eastman.

P D BARKSHIRE

RIVER VIEWS

On the image, written along the right edge: 3652- MOONRISE, CITY OF LONDON FROM WATERLOO BRIDGE. 25 JAN. 1986

1

MOONRISE
CITY OF LONDON FROM
WATERLOO BRIDGE
25 JANUARY 1986

1973-WATERLOO PIER.

28 AUG. 1982

2
WATERLOO PIER
28 AUGUST 1982

HMS Belfast
23 OCTOBER 1983

RIVER THAMES
13 AUGUST 1985

1800 – KING'S REACH MONUMENT, VICTORIA EMBANKMENT, STRAND. 29 MAY 1982

6
KING'S REACH MONUMENT
VICTORIA EMBANKMENT
29 MAY 1982

1705 – ANCHOR BREWHOUSE, BERMONDSEY.   21 APR. 1982

7
ANCHOR BREWHOUSE
BERMONDSEY
21 APRIL 1982

2252 — SHAD THAMES, BERMONDSEY.   19 MAR. 1983

8

SHAD THAMES
BERMONDSEY
19 MARCH 1983

9

BERMONDSEY WALL WEST
BERMONDSEY
19 MARCH 1983

2257 - ST. SAVIOUR'S DOCK, BERMONDSEY.

19 MAR. 1983

10
ST. SAVIOUR'S DOCK
BERMONDSEY
19 MARCH 1983

11

Chelsea Embankment
26 July 1984

VISTAS

WATLING STREET
LONDON
24 SEPTEMBER 1983

FLORAL STREET
ROSE STREET AND
GARRICK STREET
STRAND
1 JULY 1986

2566 - TENTER GROUND. SPITALFIELDS.   24 SEP. 1983

14

TENTER GROUND
SPITALFIELDS
24 SEPTEMBER 1983

3497–STAR YARD, HOLBORN.　　　　7 SEP. 1985

15
STAR YARD
HOLBORN
7 SEPTEMBER 1985

3849 – PILGRIM STREET, LONDON.   30 APR. 1986

16
PILGRIM STREET
LONDON
30 APRIL 1986

4219-CARDINAL CAP ALLEY, SOUTHWARK.   19 SEP. 1986

17
CARDINAL CAP ALLEY
SOUTHWARK
19 SEPTEMBER 1986

1005—MARLBOROUGH ROAD, ST. JAMES'S.   15 FEB. 1981

18
MARLBOROUGH ROAD
ST. JAMES'S
15 FEBRUARY 1981

BECKONING VIEWS

2034 – EATON MEWS NORTH, BELGRAVIA.   14 SEP. 1982

19

EATON MEWS NORTH
BELGRAVIA
14 SEPTEMBER 1982

20
ENTRY
LINCOLN'S INN
HOLBORN
7 JANUARY 1981

Kingly Court
Soho
3 October 1981

3556—GOODWIN'S COURT, STRAND.   29 SEP. 1985

BEDFORDBURY
↙ Nº 24   Nº 23 ↘

22
GOODWIN'S COURT
STRAND
29 SEPTEMBER 1985

38

LOCK & CO.
6 ST. JAMES'S STREET
ST. JAMES'S
16 JUNE 1979

LOCK & CO
6 ST. JAMES'S STREET
ST. JAMES'S
28 APRIL 1986

40
BERRY BROS. AND RUDD
3 ST. JAMES'S STREET
ST. JAMES'S
29 JUNE 1980

3841-BERRY BROS. & RUDD LTD, 3 ST. JAMES'S STREET, ST. JAMES'S.   28 APR. 1986

41
Berry Bros. and Rudd
3 St. James's Street
St. James's
28 April 1986

4215 — SECOND HAND BOOK SHOP, 36 GREAT QUEEN STREET, ST. GILES.   27 JUN. 1986

42
SECONDHAND BOOKSHOP
36 GREAT QUEEN STREET
ST. GILES
27 JUNE 1986

3951 – DAVIES Y SON, 32 OLD BURLINGTON STREET, MAYFAIR.   2 OCT. 1986

43
DAVIES AND SON
32 OLD BURLINGTON
STREET
MAYFAIR
2 OCTOBER 1986

Cheese Purveyors

MACE & POTTS

JOHN ADAMSON Proprietors of
PAXTON & WHITFIELD ST. JAMES. Est. 1797
Are sole suppliers of Cheese to this
establishment

44
DOOR
ESSEX STREET
STRAND
9 AUGUST 1981

972 - CHURCH BELL FOUNDRY, WHITECHAPEL ROAD, WHITECHAPEL.   13 FEB. 1981

CHURCH BELL FOUNDRY

ESTABLISHED
A.D. 1570.

45
CHURCH BELL FOUNDRY
WHITECHAPEL ROAD
WHITECHAPEL
13 FEBRUARY 1981

MODERN SHOPS

SHOP
GREAT RUSSELL STREET
BLOOMSBURY
3 SEPTEMBER 1980

SHOP
32 BEAUCHAMP PLACE
BROMPTON
23 SEPTEMBER 1986

2615-SHOP, No.187 REGENT STREET.   6 NOV.1983

49
SHOP
187 REGENT STREET
MAYFAIR
6 NOVEMBER 1983

1016 - WORKSHOP, MEARD STREET, SOHO.   17 MAR. 1981

50
WORKSHOP
MEARD STREET
SOHO
17 MARCH 1981

HIS NIBS PHILIP POOLE
182 DRURY LANE
ST. GILES
26 JUNE 1986

M322—IRONMONGERS, 14 EARLHAM STREET, ST.GILES.   1 JUL.1986

52

IRONMONGERS
14 EARLHAM STREET
ST. GILES
1 JULY 1986

PUBS

4204 - CITTIE OF YORKE, 22-23 HIGH HOLBORN, HOLBORN.   12 JUN. 1986

53
CITTIE OF YORKE
22-23 HIGH HOLBORN
HOLBORN
12 JUNE 1986

THE PRINCESS LOUISE
208 HIGH HOLBORN
ST. GILES
27 JUNE 1986

4216 – THE ANGEL, ST. GILES HIGH STREET, ST. GILES.   1 JUL. 1986

55
THE ANGEL
ST. GILES HIGH STREET
ST. GILES
1 JULY 1986

936 – THE OLD WINE SHADES, MARTIN LANE, LONDON.   31 JAN. 1981

THE OLD WINE SHADES
MARTIN LANE
LONDON
31 JANUARY 1981

57

ARCHITECTURAL DETAIL

58

RESTAURANT SIGN
GREEK STREET
SOHO
15 JUNE 1982

59

44 & 46 QUEEN ANNE'S
GATE
WESTMINSTER
23 JANUARY 1983

GIEVES & HAWKES
VIGO STREET
MAYFAIR
27 SEPTEMBER 1986

1798 – ST. PAUL'S CATHEDRAL, LONDON.   29 MAY 1982

61
ST. PAUL'S CATHEDRAL
LONDON
29 MAY 1982

DOOR
21 COLLEGE HILL
LONDON
20 FEBRUARY 1982

63
DRAPERS' HALL
THROGMORTON STREET
LONDON
9 AUGUST 1980

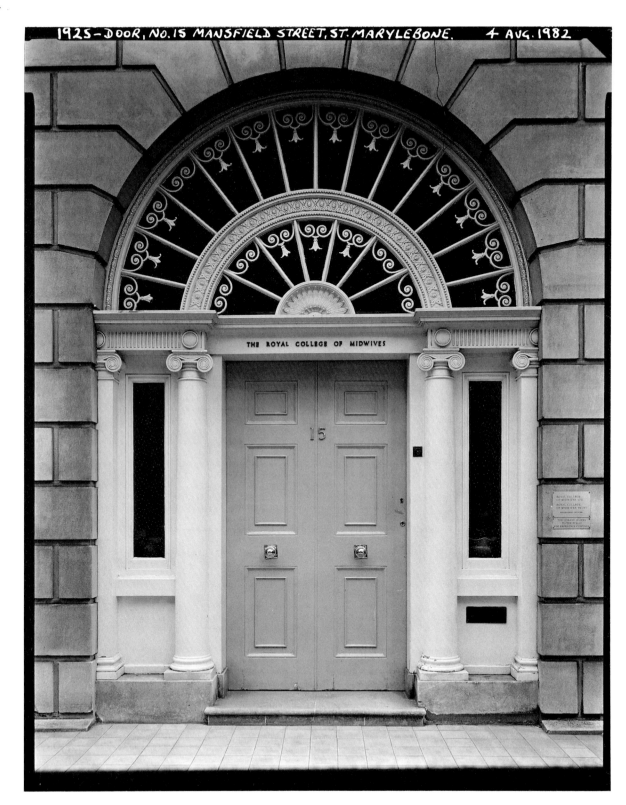

DOOR
15 MANSFIELD STREET
ST. MARYLEBONE
4 AUGUST 1982

KNOCKER
ESSEX STREET
STRAND
27 FEBRUARY 1982

FORTUNE THEATRE
RUSSELL STREET
STRAND
15 MAY 1982

SCULPTURE

WESTMINSTER BRIDGE
15 FEBRUARY 1981

3913-JAMES CORNWALL MONUMENT, SOUTH CLOISTER, WESTMINSTER ABBEY. 19 JUN. 1986

68
JAMES CORNWALL
MONUMENT
SOUTH CLOISTER
WESTMINSTER ABBEY
19 JUNE 1986

PLAQUE
GLOUCESTER GATE BRIDGE
REGENT'S PARK
9 MAY 1981

CAMBRIDGE THEATRE
SEVEN DIALS
ST. GILES
7 JULY 1982

1469-MEMORIAL, HORSE GUARDS PARADE, WHITEHALL. 25 OCT 1981

71

MEMORIAL
HORSE GUARDS PARADE
WHITEHALL
25 OCTOBER 1981

2084 - COLLEGE GARDEN, WESTMINSTER ABBEY. 11 NOV. 1982

72
COLLEGE GARDEN
WESTMINSTER ABBEY
11 NOVEMBER 1982

714 - STATUE, ST. GEORGES BURIAL GROUND, PADDINGTON STREET, ST. MARYLEBONE. 17.9.80

73
STATUE
ST. GEORGE'S BURIAL
GROUND
PADDINGTON STREET
ST. MARYLEBONE
17 SEPTEMBER 1980

2409 - STATUE, SULLIVAN MEMORIAL, VICTORIA EMBANKMENT GDS. 12·6·83

74

STATUE
THE SULLIVAN MEMORIAL
VICTORIA EMBANKMENT
GARDENS
12 JUNE 1983

DETAIL OF LAMP
TEMPLE PLACE
STRAND
28 JUNE 1983

OPEN SPACES

2240-FOUNTAIN, GREEN PARK. 7 MAR. 1983

563 - GAS LAMP, ST. JAMES'S PARK.   29 JUN. 1980

77
GAS LAMP
ST. JAMES'S PARK
29 JUNE 1980

2612 – FOUNTAIN. ST. JAMES'S PARK.

6 NOV. 1983

FOUNTAIN
ST. JAMES'S PARK
6 NOVEMBER 1983

ST. JAMES'S PARK
12 JUNE 1986

1080-FOUNTAIN, QUEEN MARY'S GARDENS, REGENTS PARK. 13 APR. 1981

80

FOUNTAIN
QUEEN MARY'S GARDENS
REGENT'S PARK
13 APRIL 1981

FOUNTAIN
KENSINGTON GARDENS
7 OCTOBER 1978

KENSINGTON GARDENS
6 FEBRUARY 1985

83
SERPENTINE BRIDGE
KENSINGTON GARDENS
27 FEBRUARY 1985

CONSTITUTION HILL
BUCKINGHAM PALACE
WESTMINSTER
15 FEBRUARY 1981

FAVOURITE PLACES

3124 - CHAPTER HOUSE, WESTMINSTER ABBEY.   9 DEC. 1984

85

CHAPTER HOUSE
WESTMINSTER ABBEY
9 DECEMBER 1984

3962 — No. 26 HAYS MEWS, MAYFAIR. 11 OCT. 1986

86
26 HAYS MEWS
MAYFAIR
11 OCTOBER 1986

3535 - BYWARD TOWER, TOWER OF LONDON.   25 SEP. 1985

87
BYWARD TOWER
TOWER OF LONDON
25 SEPTEMBER 1985

245 - PAVILION, ITALIAN GARDEN, KENSINGTON GARDENS. 16 JUNE 1979

88
PAVILION
ITALIAN GARDEN
KENSINGTON GARDENS
16 JUNE 1979

89
COURTYARD
APOTHECARIES' HALL
LONDON
30 APRIL 1986

90

Queen Anne's Gate
Westminster
19 February 1983

2414 - COURTYARD, UPPER BELGRAVE STREET, BELGRAVIA. 16 JUN. 1983

91

COURTYARD
UPPER BELGRAVE STREET
BELGRAVIA
16 JUNE 1983

2395 - GATEHOUSE, ST. BARTHOLOMEW THE GREAT, LONDON. 3 JUN. 1983

92
GATEHOUSE
ST. BARTHOLOMEW
THE GREAT
LONDON
3 JUNE 1983

Barrow Maker
Neal Street
St. Giles
23 August 1980

801 - CATHEDRAL STREET, SOUTHWARK.   26 OCT. 1980

94
CATHEDRAL STREET
SOUTHWARK
26 OCTOBER 1980

3103—No.25 FOURNIER STREET, SPITALFIELDS.   9 NOV. 1984

95

25 FOURNIER STREET
SPITALFIELDS
9 NOVEMBER 1984

96

161 DRURY LANE
ST. GILES
7 JULY 1982

2607 – No.71 SOUTH AUDLEY STREET, MAYFAIR.   30 OCT. 1983

97
71 SOUTH AUDLEY STREET
MAYFAIR
30 OCTOBER 1983

2015 — ARLINGTON STREET, ST. JAMES'S.   4 SEP. 1982

ARLINGTON STREET
ST. JAMES'S
4 SEPTEMBER 1982

M306 – CABMEN'S SHELTER, NORTHUMBERLAND AVENUE, STRAND.   12 JUN. 1986

99
CABMEN'S SHELTER
NORTHUMBERLAND
AVENUE
STRAND
12 JUNE 1986

3856 – CABMEN'S SHELTER, NORTHUMBERLAND AVENUE, STRAND.   1 MAY 1986

100
CABMEN'S SHELTER
NORTHUMBERLAND
AVENUE
STRAND
1 MAY 1986

558-CARLTON HOUSE TERRACE, THE MALL, ST. JAMES'S. 21 JUN. 1980

101
CARLTON HOUSE TERRACE
THE MALL ST. JAMES'S
21 JUNE 1980

SHOP
RUSSELL STREET
STRAND
4 APRIL 1980

1678- SEVEN STARS, CAREY STREET, HOLBORN.   18 APR. 1982

103
SEVEN STARS
CAREY STREET
HOLBORN
18 APRIL 1982

STALLS
COVENT GARDEN
SUNSET
13 NOVEMBER 1985

NOTES

RIVER VIEWS

 MOONRISE, CITY OF LONDON FROM WATERLOO BRIDGE. 25 JANUARY 1986.
This picture includes Temple Garden on the left, behind the white ship *HQS Wellington*, and the new Lloyds building on the right, behind Blackfriars Bridge. The black and white ships are *Chrysanthemum* and *President*, both due to be decommissioned. My Grandfather was a gunnery instructor on *President* at the end of the Second World War. I took the picture just after sunset to see how detailed the moon would be on a straight print.

 WATERLOO PIER. 28 AUGUST 1982.
The pier, a Thames police station, is on the north-east side of Waterloo Bridge. The dome on the right is St. Paul's Cathedral. The river police were founded in 1798, 31 years before the Metropolitan Police, to guard against ships and quays being robbed. However it wasn't the history that interested me here but the look of the back lit, white wood. The tripod had to be set up at the very edge of the pier, which was bobbing up and down. As I wanted maximum depth of field I stopped the 240mm lens right down to f/64 and risked a 3 second exposure. Only the ropes and the boat nearby are blurred, the pier and dome are sharp, so it was worth the risk.

 HMS BELFAST. 23 OCTOBER 1983.
Since this picture was taken, the quays have been demolished and most of the river bank from London Bridge to Tower Bridge has been redeveloped. *HMS Belfast*, at 11,500 tons the largest cruiser class warship built by Britain, took part in the sinking of the German battle cruiser *Scharnhorst* and opened the bombardment on D Day. It's the only British Second World War warship to be preserved. Unfortunately no First World War warships were saved, though old steam warships have been preserved by America, Russia and Japan. Taken with the 375mm lens.

 RIVER THAMES. 13 AUGUST 1985.
I took this view from almost the same point on London Bridge as the previous picture. Here I used the 300mm lens to give a wider view and include the sign. Taken at 6:30 in the morning, the picture shows the redevelopment nearly complete, and the quays just before they were demolished.

 VICTORIA EMBANKMENT, STRAND. 1 NOVEMBER 1980.
The Victoria Embankment was built 1864-1870 to the design of Sir Joseph Bazalgette. Before this, the river reached Somerset House on the left. The low arch in the middle of the arcade was the water gate. Somerset House was built 1776-1786, designed by Sir William Chambers, and is the oldest large block of government offices. The building replaced what had been the oldest English renaissance palace built 1547-1550 for Lord Protector Somerset.

 KING'S REACH MONUMENT, VICTORIA EMBANKMENT. 29 MAY 1982.
This monument at Temple Pier, where *HQS Wellington* is berthed, was built to commemorate the naming of this stretch of river King's Reach, after King George V's Silver Jubilee in 1935. In the distance is a monument to the submariners killed in the First and Second World Wars. The Embankment walls and monuments were cleaned in 1986 and this monument is now white, not black. The 30 second exposure needed to give detail to the blackness has caused some flare in the trees.

 ANCHOR BREWHOUSE, BERMONDSEY. 21 APRIL 1982.
This was taken from Tower Bridge and I can remember waiting a long time, because of wind and traffic, before exposing the film. The minimum aperture of most lenses for 8×10 format is f/64 and this often has to be used to obtain good depth of field. Even with fast film the exposures are quite long so wind and traffic are a problem. Here, using medium speed FP4 film, the exposure was ½ second at f/32 with the 240mm lens. Since this picture was taken the building has been partially demolished.

 SHAD THAMES, BERMONDSEY. 19 MARCH 1983.
This is the best street of its kind I've seen in London and the warehouses and walkways should be preserved. Shad Thames has been in many films and television programmes including *Dr. Who*.

 BERMONDSEY WALL WEST, BERMONDSEY. 19 MARCH 1983.
Looking west towards St. Saviour's Dock and Tower Bridge. The bridge is so famous that many tourists think it is London Bridge. Tower Bridge was built in 1886-1894 and is the first bridge on the Thames going up stream. I nearly didn't take this picture because it was so windy but after seeing it on the ground glass I had to risk it. I used fast HP5 film and as it was overcast exposed 2 seconds at f/64 with the 240mm lens.

 ST. SAVIOUR'S DOCK, BERMONDSEY. 19 MARCH 1983.
I like this area, which, including the dock, is being redeveloped. I hope the redevelopment is not too extensive or it will lose its Dickensian atmosphere. Just east of St. Saviour's Dock is the site of Jacob's Island, a rookery in the nineteenth century, used by Dickens as the site of Bill Sikes' death in *Oliver Twist*. At The Ship Aground, a pub in Wolseley Street on the site of Jacob's Island, there is a window painting of Bill Sikes sitting in a pub with his dog.

 CHELSEA EMBANKMENT. 26 JULY 1984.
Looking towards Battersea Bridge (built 1887-1890). The statue is by F. Derwent Wood (1871-1926). The statue was placed here to commemorate his work by members of the Chelsea Arts Club and other friends. A winter view of the same scene (*Chelsea Embankment. 18 March 1981*) is reproduced on page 307 of *The Art and Architecture of London* by Ann Saunders. Built 1871-1874, the Chelsea Embankment was designed by Sir Joseph Bazalgette, as was Battersea Bridge.

VISTAS

 WATLING STREET, LONDON. 24 SEPTEMBER 1983.
This was a road in Roman Londinium. In the distance is St. Paul's Cathedral and on the left Ye Old Watling pub. Only photographs taken in the City of London are captioned London. Places outside the City of London in Greater London are captioned with the local name. Because the City of London is changing so rapidly I often photograph there. The Guildhall Library buys nearly all the pictures I take of the City.

 FLORAL STREET, ROSE STREET & GARRICK STREET, STRAND. 1 JULY 1986.
The Strand District is the eastern part of the City of Westminster and includes Covent Garden. I've taken more pictures in the City of Westminster than any other borough or county. For this picture I used Gravure Positive, a slow blue sensitive film, that I often use on overcast days for its higher contrast. The exposure was 6 seconds at f/32 with the 155mm lens. (The building with the balustrades is the Garrick Club.)

 TENTER GROUND, SPITALFIELDS. 24 SEPTEMBER 1983.
Here I was just as interested in the light as the group of buildings. The buildings on the left have been demolished. Spitalfields is in the London Borough of Tower Hamlets whose local history library buys many of the pictures I take in the borough. The Bishopsgate Institute also buys pictures taken in this borough. The street name Tenter Ground reflects the importance of the weaving industry in the history of Spitalfields.

STAR YARD, HOLBORN.
7 SEPTEMBER 1985.
The large building with the tower in the distance is The Royal Courts of Justice, usually called the Law Courts, on the Strand. It was built 1871-1882. The boundary between the City of Westminster and the London Borough of Camden runs down the middle of Star Yard. Holborn is in the London Borough of Camden.

 PILGRIM STREET, LONDON.
30 APRIL 1986.
The church is St. Martin's, built after the Great Fire in 1666 and designed by Sir Christopher Wren, on Ludgate Hill. I'd been using Tri-X Pan film since the summer of 1984. In April 1986, as I was now sure of a steady supply of the film as it is imported from America, I did a series of exposure and development tests for normal, high and low contrast. After these tests I could take this picture with confidence knowing I would get a detailed black in shadow and a detailed white in sunlight.

 CARDINAL CAP ALLEY, SOUTHWARK.
19 SEPTEMBER 1986.
The old house is No.1 Cardinal's Wharf and is across the River Thames from St. Paul's Cathedral. According to tradition Sir Christopher Wren lived here while his St. Paul's Cathedral was being built 1675-1710. For this picture I used Tri-X Ortho (sensitive to blue and green but not red) to lighten the foliage. As this film is not sold here I order it from my brother in Canada.

 MARLBOROUGH ROAD, ST. JAMES'S. 15 FEBRUARY 1981.
The gate in the distance is on The Mall and leads into St. James's Park. On the right is St. James's Palace built in the 1530s during the reign of King Henry VIII. It became the official residence of the sovereign after Whitehall Palace burned down in 1698. The building on the left is the Queen's Chapel, designed by Inigo Jones, and built in the 1620s for Henrietta Maria, the wife of Charles I.

BECKONING VIEWS

 EATON MEWS NORTH, BELGRAVIA.
14 SEPTEMBER 1982.
Belgravia was developed from 1825-1855 by Thomas Cubitt whose main architect was George Basevi, a pupil of Sir John Soane. It's the most expensive area of London and was built to rival Mayfair. After taking this picture I was reminded of a photograph by Francis Frith taken in 1858 of the Mosque of El-Hakim in Cairo. I rarely consciously make cover versions and it's usually some time after taking a picture that I realise it's a cover version.

 ENTRY, LINCOLN'S INN, HOLBORN. 7 JANUARY 1981.
Taken from Carey Street just around the corner from Star Yard. This archway was built in 1697 and is one of the three main entrances to Lincoln's Inn. Through the archway is New Square, one of London's best, with many fine old buildings. The four Inns of Court, Middle Temple, Inner Temple, Lincoln's Inn and Gray's Inn, were founded in the late thirteenth or early fourteenth century to serve as a university of the law, where lawyers and students could live and study.

 KINGLY COURT, SOHO.
3 OCTOBER 1981.
Soho was developed from the early seventeenth century. Many aristocratic mansions were built at that time but none have survived. Through the archway is Upper John Street, leading to Soho's first square, Golden Square, built in 1681. Further on in Lower John Street is an old house built in 1685, probably the oldest house in Soho as none of the earlier houses have survived. Although Soho is in central London many modest eighteenth-century houses, like the backs of the houses in this picture, still exist.

 GOODWIN'S COURT, STRAND. 29 SEPTEMBER 1985.
A view of this alley taken in the opposite direction *(Goodwin's Court, Strand. 17 August 1981)* is reproduced on page 123 of *The Art and Architecture of London*. Goodwin's Court is between Bedfordbury and St. Martin's Lane with covered archways at each end. Although I'd photographed this archway twice before, in 1981 and 1982, I hadn't included the reflector shown in this picture. These reflectors, to increase the light in ground floor rooms, were once common in London's alleyways but this is the only one I've seen.

 BRYDGES PLACE, STRAND.
7 AUGUST 1982.
Looking towards St. Martin's Lane. This bleak, narrow, slightly sinister alley also runs from Bedfordbury to St. Martin's Lane. Though very different to Goodwin's Court, just to the north, it is just as attractive to photograph because of its special quality. To make a portrait of London that includes only the obviously notable and beautiful would not only be untrue but wouldn't be as much fun to work on.

 GATE, PEARL ASSURANCE CO. LTD., HIGH HOLBORN.
14 NOVEMBER 1982.
The Pearl Assurance Company building was built in 1912. In the courtyard beyond the ornate gate is a statue of St. George. High Holborn is a section of the Roman road that runs from Newgate in the City of London to Staines. Holborn was London's smallest borough before it became part of the London Borough of Camden in 1965, when the county of Greater London was created.

 ROYAL OPERA ARCADE, ST. JAMES'S. 3 SEPTEMBER 1982.
This is London's oldest, and best, arcade. It was built 1816-1818 to the design of John Nash and G.S. Repton, and now runs through a modern building that I hate – New Zealand House. There is nothing wrong with this 15-storey building in itself but it ruins so many views that I wish it had been built somewhere else. I plan to photograph modern architecture in London including historic views spoilt by modern buildings. The arcade wasn't empty when I took this picture but as the exposure was 16 minutes nobody was still long enough to register on the film.

INTERIORS

 CLOISTER, MERCHANT TAYLORS' HALL, LONDON.
23 APRIL 1986.
There was so much of interest in the Merchant Taylors' Hall that I needed two days to photograph it, taking nine pictures on 18 April and eleven pictures on 23 April. The City Companies developed from the medieval craft and trade guilds. Many of their halls were destroyed in the Great Fire in 1666 and again in the Second World War, but the Merchant Taylors' Hall, on this site since 1347, was only partly damaged in both these calamities.

 STAIRS, DR. JOHNSON'S HOUSE, GOUGH SQUARE, LONDON. 3 MAY 1985.
Dr. Johnson lived in this smart late seventeenth-century house from 1748-1759, while he wrote the *Dictionary*, and it was here his wife died from drink and opium in 1752. One of his most famous remarks is 'When a man is tired of London, he is tired of life, for there is in London all that life can afford.' Although Johnson lived in many houses in London, this is the only one of his houses remaining. It was bought by Lord Harmsworth in 1911 and after restoration given to the nation.

 CONVEX MIRROR, GREAT PARLOUR, MERCHANT TAYLORS' HALL. 18 APRIL 1986.
The Merchant Taylors' Hall has rooms dating from several different centuries, including a late fourteenth-century crypt and the Great Kitchen, in use since 1427. This view of an opulent mirror in the Great Parlour, shows my camera and tripod reflected.

STAIRS, ELY HOUSE, 37 DOVER STREET, MAYFAIR.
25 JUNE 1985.
Built in 1772, to the design of Sir Robert Taylor, it was the town house of the Bishops of Ely. I've also wanted to photograph the neat Palladian facade for years but either the light hasn't been right or there have been cars in the way whenever I've been there. The horseshoe stairs were made in 1909 when the house was enlarged, to the design of A. Dunbar Smith and Cecil Brewer, for the Albemarle Club.

30

SCREEN, MIDDLE TEMPLE HALL, LONDON.
4 APRIL 1986.
This fine oak Renaissance screen was well restored after bomb damage in the Second World War. The Hall, with a double hammerbeam roof, was built in 1562-1570. The four Inns of Court are halfway between the commercial centre in the City of London and the political centre in Westminster. Inner Temple and Middle Temple are on land once owned by the Order of the Knights Templars founded in 1118 and dissolved in 1312, when the Knights of St. John took over the land and leased some of it to lawyers.

 31

PRINCE HENRY'S ROOM, 17 FLEET STREET, LONDON.
14 MAY 1986.
I'd tried to photograph this interior in 1983 with the 240mm lens, but during the 6 minute exposure the heavy traffic in Fleet Street gave a blurred negative. Though there was heavy traffic on the day I took this second picture, with the wider 155mm lens, I managed to get a sharp picture with a 3 minute exposure by closing the shutter when I could hear a bus or taxi approaching. After the traffic passed I opened the shutter and by this method gradually built up the 3 minute exposure. This fine old house was build in 1610-1611 as an inn and the ceiling commemorates Prince Henry, son of James I, becoming Prince of Wales in 1610.

 32

BILL STICKERS RESTAURANT/BAR, 18 GREEK STREET, SOHO.
28 JUNE 1986.
Soho became established as an entertainment centre in the middle of the nineteenth century with theatres, music halls and prostitutes, but did not become the gastronomic centre it now is until after the First World War. During the summer of 1986, though I photographed a few historic interiors, I concentrated very much on shop, pub and restaurant interiors. Bill Stickers had just opened when I photographed the bizarre interior and work was still going on.

 33

STAIRS, 66 BROOK STREET, MAYFAIR. 18 JUNE 1985.
I took two over-all views of these stairs but not being happy with either I took this detail, by far the best picture. This house and 53 Davies Street around the corner is the Grosvenor Office. The Grosvenor Estate, owned by the Duke of Westminster, includes much of Mayfair and Belgravia, the most expensive districts of London. Mayfair was developed from the 1660s to the 1750s and became London's aristocratic centre, taking over from the declining Soho and Covent Garden, and unlike those districts did not decline when the fashionable Belgravia was built.

 34

STAIRCASE, HOUSE OF ST. BARNABAS, SOHO.
21 JULY 1983.

 35

CEILING, HOUSE OF ST. BARNABAS, 1 GREEK STREET, SOHO.
14 JULY 1985.
I was asked to photograph this interior for Victoria Library in July 1983. This was two years before I concentrated on historic London interiors and then I didn't know the full historic importance of this interior. In 1985, when I knew this type of interior was not common, I returned to take details of the superb plasterwork. The artists who made this plasterwork in the mid eighteenth century are not known. In 1861 the houses was sold to the House of St. Barnabas in Soho, a charity founded in 1846 for the relief of the homeless poor of London.

 36

ST. BARTHOLOMEW THE GREAT, LITTLE BRITAIN, LONDON. 12 JULY 1980.
Although the nave was demolished after the Reformation the choir became a parish church. It was built from 1132 when Rahere founded an Augustinian priory and is the oldest church in London except for the chapel in the Tower. The atmosphere of this church, where William Hogarth was baptised in 1697, is quite different from churches built in later centuries in London. I was using slow Ilford Ortho film at this time and the exposure was 1½ hours. Just after I opened the shutter the tripod was kicked so the windows are blurred but the rest of the picture is sharp.

HISTORIC SHOPS

 37

NEWSAGENTS, 88 DEAN STREET, SOHO. 17 JUNE 1986.
I've photographed this unique Rococo shop front, built c.1791, three times. When I took the first picture, in 1982, there was an ugly modern sign above the shop door. When I discovered the sign had been removed, I photographed the shop early in the morning of the 13 June 1986, when it was closed and when there were bundles of newspapers on the ground, but after processing the negative I decided the picture wasn't good enough and returned to take this closer view.

 38

LOCK & CO., 6 ST. JAMES'S STREET, ST. JAMES'S.
16 JUNE 1979.

 39

LOCK & CO., 6 ST. JAMES'S STREET, ST. JAMES'S.
28 APRIL 1986.
Lock & Co. moved to this shop in 1764 from a shop across the street where they started in 1676. The business was started by Robert Davis and passed to his son Charles after his death in 1696. In turn, Charles Davis's son-in-law James Lock inherited the business in 1759. At the back of the shop is a small courtyard with an old cottage, while upstairs is the Nelson Room. Nelson and the Duke of Wellington both bought hats from this shop.

 40

BERRY BROS. & RUDD LTD., 3 ST. JAMES'S STREET, ST. JAMES'S. 29 JUNE 1980.

 41

BERRY BROS. & RUDD LTD., 3 ST. JAMES'S STREET, ST. JAMES'S. 28 APRIL 1986.
The shop front was built in the second half of the eighteenth century and the interior has an incredibly sloping floor. Widow Bourne started a grocery shop here in about 1699 that was later taken over by William Pickering her son-in-law. On the left of the shop is a covered passage that leads to Pickering Place, a courtyard of old houses, built by William Pickering in the 1730s. The grocery business was stopped at the end of the nineteenth century when the firm continued as wine merchants.

 42

SECOND HAND BOOK SHOP, 36 GREAT QUEEN STREET, ST. GILES. 27 JUNE 1986.
Great Queen Street was built in the 1630s, though none of the original houses remain. There are some old houses in the street, built in the early eighteenth century, including this shop. For a second hand book shop it has a very elegant interior, though the booksellers, Horace C. Blossom, think it is a nineteenth-century interior in the style of the eighteenth century. Because of the high contrast, I gave the film twice the normal exposure and less than normal development.

 43

DAVIES & SON, 32 OLD BURLINGTON STREET, MAYFAIR. 2 OCTOBER 1986.
Though October is rather late in the year to photograph interiors, there was enough light from the large window for a 70 second exposure at f/40 with the 155mm lens. The tailors Davies & Son were founded in 1803 and had a shop in Hanover Street until 1980, when they moved to this old house. Old Burlington Street, on the Burlington Estate, was built from 1718 and No.32 is one of the original houses.

44

DOOR, ESSEX STREET, STRAND. 9 AUGUST 1981.
The sign is not old but its style is and as there are no old signs in London I photographed this as an example. Essex Street was developed in the 1680s after Essex House was demolished in 1674. In the sixteenth and early seventeenth centuries, large aristocratic mansions were built along the south side of the Strand, with gardens and terraces going down to the river, from The Temple to Charing Cross. They were demolished one by one from the late seventeenth century, until the last of the great mansions, Northumberland House, was demolished in 1874.

 45

CHURCH BELL FOUNDRY, WHITECHAPEL ROAD, WHITECHAPEL.
13 FEBRUARY 1981.
The shop front has been tarted up since this picture was taken and the wood shop front has lost its patina. The foundry moved to this site in 1738, taking over the buildings of the seventeenth-century Artichoke Inn, and since its establishment in 1570 many famous bells have been made there, including those for Westminster Abbey, Big Ben, and the Liberty Bell and the Bicentennial Bell, both in America.

MODERN SHOPS

 46

SHOP, GREAT RUSSELL STREET, BLOOMSBURY.
3 SEPTEMBER 1980.
It was pure luck that this shop was across from the British Museum so that I could make this joke picture. The shop changed from a novelties shop to a clothes shop a few years after I took it. Great Russell Street and Russell Street are both named after the Russells, Dukes of Bedford, who owned land in Bloomsbury and Covent Garden. The British Museum was built in 1823-1852 to the design of Sir Robert Smirke.

 47

SHOP, 32 BEAUCHAMP PLACE, BROMPTON.
23 SEPTEMBER 1986.
Brompton and Chelsea are both districts in The Royal Borough of Kensington and Chelsea and though there is much of interest in the borough I rarely photograph there. I'd noticed this shop a few days before I took this picture but the street, as is usual in a busy area close to Harrod's, was full of parked cars and their reflections ruined my attempts. I returned early in the morning of 23 September and got the picture I wanted.

 48

SHOP, PICCADILLY, ST. JAMES'S. 3 NOVEMBER 1982.
I find shop windows fascinating, not just because they are visually interesting but because they often say something about the society they serve. Though Piccadilly is one of the ancient roads entering London from the west, building did not begin on the street until the early seventeenth century. In the eighteenth and nineteenth centuries it was a fashionable street with fine mansions, but these have nearly all been demolished and replaced with offices, hotels and shops.

 49

SHOP, 187 REGENT STREET, MAYFAIR. 6 NOVEMBER 1983.
When I saw this shop I got an immediate message from the combination of open mouthed children and birds and had to take this ugly picture. Regent Street was laid out in 1813-1825 to the design of John Nash as part of the route from Carlton House to Regent's Park. the original buildings have all been demolished and replaced with twentieth-century buildings, but the street, as it was designed to, still separates Soho and Mayfair.

 50

WORKSHOP, MEARD STREET, SOHO. 17 MARCH 1981.
This was the workshop of H. Peen, boot tree, shoe tree and last makers, who have now moved as Soho is declining into a new fashionable phase. Meard Street is a short pedestrian street, running from Dean Street to Wardour Street, with fine simple Georgian houses built in 1722-1732 by the carpenter John Meard. The sex shops and the gentrification of Soho have increased rents to the point where other shops and workshops have had to move.

 51

HIS NIBS PHILIP POOLE, 182 DRURY LANE, ST. GILES.
26 JUNE 1986.
As I needed good depth of field for this picture I closed down the 155mm lens to f/50 so that the exposure was 6 minutes. During the exposure people came in the shop, so I had to close the shutter and open it after they left to continue the exposure. Before Aldwych and Kingsway were laid out in 1900-1905 Drury Lane was the main road from the Strand to Oxford Street. There were some very old houses in Drury Lane in the nineteenth century and Wych Street, destroyed when Aldwych was laid out, had a complete row of Tudor houses.

 52

IRONMONGERS, 14 EARLHAM STREET, ST. GILES.
1 JULY 1986.
While setting up this picture I was reminded of Atget's PP380-*Rue de La Reynie, étameur,* taken in Paris in 1912. If I were photographing for art's sake alone I wouldn't have taken this picture, because it is not original, but I don't care about such things. I like this picture as much as Atget's and if I were bothered about originality I probably wouldn't photograph London at all.

PUBS

 53

CITTIE OF YORKE, 22-23 HIGH HOLBORN, HOLBORN.
12 JUNE 1986.
This part of the pub was built in 1430, though rebuilt with some of the original materials in 1923. Until recently the pub was called Henekey's Long Bar because it was one of the longest bars in Britain, but after it was shortened the name was changed. On the right, not shown in the picture, are booths built so lawyers and their clients can speak privately. The pub is next to the High Holborn gatehouse of Gray's Inn. Note the old large vats on the gallery and the three cornered fireplace that has a chimney under the floor.

 54

THE PRINCESS LOUISE, 208 HIGH HOLBORN, ST. GILES.
27 JUNE 1986.
This fine Victorian pub is in the St. Giles section of High Holborn. St. Giles is west and Holborn is east of Kingsway. One of the customers foolishly tried to keep still during the 6 minute exposure; he probably thought it would take a few seconds. Photographing people with the 8×10 is a bit of a problem because of the slow shutter speeds, but if they are not the subject I don't mind blurred people and 'ghosts'.

 55

THE ANGEL, ST. GILES HIGH STREET, ST. GILES.
1 JULY 1986.
In the summer of 1985 when I was photographing historic interiors I didn't have a wide angle lens, just the semi-wide 240mm lens, and I couldn't take many pictures that I wanted to. In August, after trying to find a second-hand wide angle, I asked the people at Teamwork if they would buy a new lens for me and I would pay them over two years. They asked me to come back in a few days so they could think about it. I thought that meant no, but when I went back to the shop they bought a 155mm Redenstock for me and I used it for most of the interiors photographed in 1986.

 56

THE CROSS KEYS, ENDELL STREET, ST. GILES.
18 AUGUST 1980.
During the summer of 1980 I was using slow Ilford Ortho film and I think the man in the top window must have been determined to have his picture taken, as the exposure was 3 seconds at f/45 with the 375mm lens. Endell Street (the next street east of Neal Street) has some buildings I still haven't photographed yet, because of parked cars in the way. St. Giles, formerly in the borough of Holborn, is the southernmost district of the London Borough of Camden.

57

THE OLD WINE SHADES, MARTIN LANE, LONDON.
31 JANUARY 1981.
Built in 1663, this pub incredibly survived the Fire though just a few streets from Pudding Lane where the Fire started in the early morning of 2 September 1666. In the strong wind, the fire spread rapidly and in four days destroyed four-fifths of the City. Although medieval London was destroyed in the fire the street plan remained the same and has changed hardly at all since. There were plans to redesign the street plan of the City after the fire but land ownership and the need to rebuild quickly meant that the old streets were kept to.

ARCHITECTURAL DETAIL

 58

RESTAURANT SIGN, GREEK STREET, SOHO. 15 JUNE 1982.
Greek Street was built at the end of the seventeenth century and there are still some early eighteenth-century houses in the street. The sign, made around 1927, shows the owner of L'Escargot at that time, Georges Gaudin, who established the restaurant. When I took a print of this to L'Escargot I was told the council had told them to remove the sign. With all the cheap mass produced signs in London there should be more original signs like this, not less. The owners refused to remove the sign and it is still there.

44 & 46 QUEEN ANNE'S GATE, WESTMINSTER.
23 JANUARY 1983.
These houses were built at the beginning of the eighteenth century. The great advantage of view cameras for architectural photography, besides the detail from the large format, is the camera movements. By raising the lens the back of the camera can be kept level to avoid converging verticals. The covering power of each lens determines to what extent the camera movements can be used. For this picture the lens was raised so high that the top corners are outside the circle of good definition but I was more interested in the overall look of the picture than the details.

 GIEVES & HAWKES, VIGO STREET, MAYFAIR.
27 SEPTEMBER 1986.
I thought the receding windows strange, and as the light was good I decided this picture was worth taking. This house was built at the end of the seventeenth century and the tailors Gieves & Hawkes founded in 1771. As Vigo Street is narrow I had to use the wide angle 155mm lens raised to maximum height. This lens, unlike the 240mm used in the view of Queen Anne's Gate has great covering power and the top of the picture is sharp as it is inside the circle of good definition.

 ST. PAUL'S CATHEDRAL, LONDON. 29 MAY 1982.
On this site was a Roman Temple of Diana and the first St. Paul's Cathedral was built in 604. It was rebuilt in stone in 675-685 but this second building was burned down by Vikings in 961. The third Saxon cathedral burned down in a fire that destroyed a large part of the City in 1087. When the subsequent Romanesque and Gothic cathedral was completed 'Old St. Paul's' was one of the largest buildings in Europe and was considerably larger than the modern cathedral. This was built in 1675-1710 after the medieval cathedral was destroyed in the Great Fire.

 DOOR, 21 COLLEGE HILL, LONDON. 20 FEBRUARY 1982.
The fine, late seventeenth-century gateways at 21 and 22a College Hill are the only ones of this style in London. The carving under the canopy of No.22a is different to that of No.21. London's most famous Lord Mayor Sir Richard Whittington had a house built on this street and paid for the rebuilding of St. Michael Paternoster Royal where he was buried in 1423.

 DRAPERS' HALL, THROGMORTON STREET, LONDON. 9 AUGUST 1980.
The first Lord Mayor of London William FitzAlwyn, Lord Mayor from 1192-1212, was a member of the Drapers' Company. In 1541 the Drapers moved to this site taking over Thomas Cromwell's house. They bought the mansion from Henry VIII after Cromwell was executed in 1540 and built a new Hall after the Fire of 1666. The Hall was again rebuilt when a fire in 1772 destroyed all but the Court Dining Room and the Clerks' Office, which were preserved.

 DOOR, 15 MANSFIELD STREET, ST. MARYLEBONE.
4 AUGUST 1982.
There are so many fine eighteenth-century doors in London the problem is how many to photograph. After photographing various typical doors for my collection I now photograph those I find particularly striking. The old houses in Mansfield Street were built in 1772 by the Adam brothers and the street is named after Viscount Mansfield, Duke of Newcastle. The former boroughs of St. Marylebone and Paddington became part of the City of Westminster in 1965.

 KNOCKER, ESSEX STREET, STRAND. 27 FEBRUARY 1982.
This evil-looking knocker could be 300 years old, as Essex Street was developed then on the site of Essex House. A great advantage of using view cameras is that close ups can be taken without a special lens, because the lens is attached to a bellows. When the bellows are extended so that the distance from the film to the lens is twice the focal length, then the image is the same size as the object.

 FORTUNE THEATRE, RUSSELL STREET, STRAND.
15 MAY 1982.
I'd photographed this front from the same position in 1980 with the wider angle 240mm lens. Then when I heard the theatre was going to be demolished I took this closer view with the 375mm lens. The picture was taken from the roof of the colonnade of Drury Lane Theatre Royal. The Fortune Theatre was built in 1924 to the design of Ernest Schaufelberg, who was the sculptor of this nude, and luckily the plans to redevelop the site were scrapped.

SCULPTURE

 WESTMINSTER BRIDGE.
15 FEBRUARY 1981.
The plaque says 'This lion modelled by W.F. Woodington and made in Coades artificial stone stood from 1837 on the parapet above the river front of the Lion Brewery Lambeth. It survived the surrounding devastation in the war of 1939-45 and when the site was cleared for the building of the Royal Festival Hall, was preserved in accordance with the wishes of His Majesty King George VI.' Westminster Bridge was built in 1854-1862 to replace the first Westminster Bridge built in 1738-1749.

 JAMES CORNWALL MONUMENT, SOUTH CLOISTER, WESTMINSTER ABBEY. 19 JUNE 1986.
This fine monument is just inside the Dean's Yard entrance. According to tradition the first church on this site, then called Thorny Island because it was surrounded by water, was built in the early seventh century. A Benedictine abbey was founded here in the first half of the eighth century and called Westminster because it was to the west of the City of London. The abbey was rebuilt in the Romanesque style by Edward the Confessor and consecrated by him in 1065. Edward was canonized in 1163 and in his honour Henry III had the abbey rebuilt in the French style to the design of Henry of Reims 1245-1269. The nave was completed in the same style by Henry Yevele in 1376-1388. Later additions are the Henry VII Chapel built in the early sixteenth century and the twin west towers built in the eighteenth century by Nicholas Hawksmoor.

 PLAQUE, GLOUCESTER GATE BRIDGE, REGENT'S PARK.
9 MAY 1981.
This plaque is not in the park but in the district east of the park also called Regent's Park. According to tradition St. Pancras was martyred during the reign of the Roman Emperor Diocletian (284-305). Surrounding the park are grand terraces and houses, most of which were designed by John Nash and built circa 1825.

 CAMBRIDGE THEATRE, SEVEN DIALS, ST. GILES.
7 JULY 1982.
The theatre was built in 1930 by the architectural partnership of Wimperis, Simpson and Guthrie. Seven Dials was developed at the end of the seventeenth century by Thomas Neal as a fashionable area but it soon became one of the worst slums in London. The area is shown in Hogarth's engraving *Gin Lane* (1751) and described in Charles Dickens's *Sketches by Boz* and *Bleak House*. Seven Dials is being redeveloped and many of the old houses restored.

 MEMORIAL, HORSE GUARDS PARADE, WHITEHALL.
25 OCTOBER 1981.
This is the Cadiz Memorial set up to commemorate the raising of the seige of Cadiz by the Duke of Wellington on 22 July 1812. It is a French mortar cannon, resting on a cast iron Chinese dragon. Behind the Cadiz Memorial is the Horse Guards built in 1750-1758 to the design of William Kent. The Horse Guards Parade is on the site of the tilt-yard of Whitehall Palace which burned down in 1698.

COLLEGE GARDEN, WESTMINSTER ABBEY. 11 NOVEMBER 1982.
This is probably the oldest continually cultivated garden in England. The eighteenth-century statues have been badly damaged by pollution. Behind them is the fourteenth-century abbey precinct wall.
The steps lead to Great College Street, thought to mark the southern boundary of Thorny Island, built c.1722 with some of the original houses remaining.

STATUE, ST. GEORGE'S BURIAL GROUND, PADDINGTON STREET, ST. MARYLEBONE. 17 SEPTEMBER 1980.
Now a public garden, this was St. George's burial ground from 1731-1851. The nineteenth-century statue by Donato Bareaglia is called The Street Orderly Boy and has been in the garden since 1943.
St. Marylebone was developed in the eighteenth century and there are many fine streets and houses of that time. Before then it was a village on the Tyburn stream now covered over, though its course can be followed from the meanderings of Marylebone High Street and Marylebone Lane.

STATUE, THE SULLIVAN MEMORIAL, VICTORIA EMBANKMENT GARDENS. 12 JUNE 1983.
The monument to Sir Arthur Sullivan, who wrote the music for the Gilbert and Sullivan operettas, has on its plinth 'Is life a boon?; If so it must befall; That death when e'er he call; Must call too soon', written by W.S. Gilbert. Victoria Embankment Gardens were built on land reclaimed from the Thames after the embankment was built 1864-1870. The gardens have many statues and monuments, as well as the York Watergate built in 1626.

DETAIL OF LAMP, TEMPLE PLACE, STRAND. 28 JUNE 1983.
This is a detail of one of the two bronze lamps by W.S. Frith at 2 Temple Place. The house was built for William Waldorf Astor in 1895 and the architect was John Loughborough Pearson (1817-1898). It was called Astor House and has an extraordinary interior with fine floors, stairs and carvings. Usually I close down the lens so everything is sharp but for this picture I closed down the lens just enough for the depth of field to cover the lamp and leave the background out of focus.

OPEN SPACES

FOUNTAIN, GREEN PARK. 7 MARCH 1983.
Green Park was made a Royal Park by Charles II and opened to the public. In the eighteenth century it was a favourite place for duels, firework displays, ballooning and highwaymen. The Diana Fountain by E.J. Clack was placed in Green Park in 1954.

GAS LAMP, ST. JAMES'S PARK. 29 JUNE 1980.

FOUNTAIN, ST. JAMES'S PARK. 6 NOVEMBER 1983.

ST. JAMES'S PARK. 12 JUNE 1986
The park was a marshy field until King Henry VIII had it drained and turned it into a deer park. Charles II had the park laid out in the French formal style and opened it to the public. Several small ponds were made into a lake with straight sides called The Canal and this was made to look like a natural lake in 1826-1827. The photograph of the lake is a cover version of Atget's LD1001 - Parc, La Malmaison (taken c.1920) and is one of the few cover versions I've consciously taken.

FOUNTAIN, QUEEN MARY'S GARDENS, REGENT'S PARK. 13 APRIL 1981.
Queen Mary's Gardens are inside the Inner Circle and the Triton Fountain was made in 1939 by William Macmillan. Regent's Park was developed in the early nineteenth century and most of it had been opened to the public bv 1841. In the park are the Zoological Gardens opened in 1828 and now a major tourist attraction in London. These Royal Parks, Regent's, St. James's, Green and Hyde form an important part of London's character.

FOUNTAIN, KENSINGTON GARDENS. 7 OCTOBER 1978.

KENSINGTON GARDENS. 6 FEBRUARY 1985.
Kensington Gardens and the adjoining Hyde Park form the largest park in central London with about 635 acres. The Italian Water Garden was built in 1861. Hyde Park was opened to the public by King James I and Kensington Gardens was opened to the public all year round by King William IV. The photograph of the fountain is the first I took in London with the 8×10 camera.

SERPENTINE BRIDGE, KENSINGTON GARDENS. 27 FEBRUARY 1985.
The elegant Serpentine Bridge by George Rennie was built in 1826. A few days before I took the picture of the bridge, I'd set up this picture but the light wasn't right. While climbing over the fence I dropped and smashed the old Eastman View No.2 and though I managed to fix it when I got home it was in a poor condition. The camera was about 60 years old and always difficult to use, so in August 1985, with money from the 1986 *Popular Photography Annual*, I bought a new Wista Field DX 8×10 camera.

CONSTITUTION HILL, BUCKINGHAM PALACE, WESTMINSTER. 15 FEBRUARY 1981.
Constitution Hill runs between Buckingham Palace and Green Park and is thought to have been named from King Charles II's habit of walking here. In the centre distance is the Queen Victoria Memorial by Thomas Brock, who was knighted there by King George V at its unveiling in 1911.

FAVOURITE PLACES

CHAPTER HOUSE, WESTMINSTER ABBEY. 9 DECEMBER 1984.
The graceful flying buttresses, though they look integral to the building, were built in the middle of the fourteenth century, 100 years after the Chapter House was built. The Great Council met here in 1257 and from 1352-1547 it was used as the House of Commons so the building has been called the 'cradle of all free parliaments'. After 1547 the House of Commons met in nearby St. Stephen's Chapel, in the Palace of Westminster, and the Chapter House was used to store State papers until 1866.

26 HAYS MEWS, MAYFAIR. 11 OCTOBER 1986.
This mid eighteenth-century house was probably the workshop of the master carpenter John Phillips, who built most of the houses in nearby Charles Street. I'd photographed this weather-boarded house twice before, in 1981 and 1983, and for this picture I used Tri-X Ortho to lighten the green painted boards. With Ortho film green is about half a stop lighter than Pan film, blue one stop lighter, red one stop darker, and yellow half a stop darker.

BYWARD TOWER, TOWER OF LONDON. 25 SEPTEMBER 1985.
The Tower of London is one of the best fortresses in England and if the moat hadn't been drained and the stone cleaned it would be even better. A temporary fort was built here in 1067 by William the Conqueror and this was replaced by the White Tower built 1078-1097. Most of the rest of the Tower, the inner and outer walls with their towers, was built in the reigns of Henry III (1216-72) and Edward I (1272-1307). Each tower is visually different and has its own history. The Byward (meaning password) Tower was built during the reign of Edward I and altered later in the fourteenth century.

PAVILION, ITALIAN GARDEN, KENSINGTON GARDENS. 16 JUNE 1979.
The former Pumping Station, now the Pavilion, said to have been designed by Prince Albert. I like its fine detail and its typical Victorian neatness.

COURTYARD, APOTHECARIES' HALL, LONDON. 30 APRIL 1986.
At 12 Black Friars Lane the site was bought by the Apothecaries' Society in 1632. The old buildings, formerly the guest house of the Dominican priory, were destroyed in the Fire. The Hall was built c.1670 and further building in 1786 made this courtyard. The Apothecaries split from the Grocers and received their first charter from James I in 1617. The lamp in the courtyard is over a thirteenth-century well.

QUEEN ANNE'S GATE, WESTMINSTER.
19 FEBRUARY 1983.
These old stone banded houses were built at the beginning of the eighteenth century. Until 1873 there was a wall across the street where the statue of Queen Anne stands. This part of the street was called Queen Square and beyond the wall, Park Street. Most of the houses in the former Park Street were built later in the eighteenth century. This is one of London's best streets and many famous people have lived here, including Lord Palmerston and Lord Fisher.

91 COURTYARD, UPPER BELGRAVE STREET, BELGRAVIA. 16 JUNE 1983.
Although Belgravia is one of the most expensive districts of London most of these courtyards are bare and shabby. Before Belgravia was developed in the second quarter of the nineteenth century it was mostly fields with isolated groups of houses. Some of these eighteenth-century houses remain including the house where Mozart lived. The name Belgravia comes from the Grosvenor estate at Belgrave in Cheshire.

92 GATEHOUSE, ST. BARTHOLOMEW THE GREAT, LONDON.
3 JUNE 1983.
This is one of the few sixteenth-century houses to have survived in central London. Most were destroyed in the Great Fire in 1666 and the Victorians demolished nearly all the ancient houses that survived the Fire. The house is built over a thirteenth-century arched doorway that was the south door of the nave of St. Bartholomew the Great. The nave, built c.1230-1240, was demolished when the Augustinian Priory became a parish church.

93 BARROW MAKER, NEAL STREET, ST. GILES.
23 AUGUST 1980.
This is another of the many shops I've photographed that has closed since my visit. Neal Street is just north of Covent Garden and after the vegetable market moved to Nine Elms in 1973, the area became very gentrified. I'd walked past this shop many times but it wasn't until I saw the rhythmic row of barrows outside that I had to photograph it.

94 CATHEDRAL STREET, SOUTHWARK.
26 OCTOBER 1980.
Looking towards St. Mary Overy's wharf. This area just west of Southwark Cathedral has changed a lot in the seven years since this picture was taken. The distant warehouse on the Thames is now a pub, and there are modern offices on both sides of the road, with a covered walkway between them. The surface of the road has remained the same and the bollards are still there. Although I've only been photographing London since 1978, so many places and buildings I've photographed have been demolished or altered.

95 25 FOURNIER STREET, SPITALFIELDS.
9 NOVEMBER 1984.
In 1685 Louis XIV revoked the Edict of Nantes which had given French Protestants freedom of worship in 1598. About 30,000 Huguenots came to England and many of them, who were skilled silk weavers, settled in Spitalfields. This old house and others in Fournier Street (and other streets in the area) have wide windows in the garrets that were used as workshops. Although this is a poor district these old houses are fashionable and many have been restored recently.

96 161 DRURY LANE, ST. GILES.
7 JULY 1982.
This is another house I liked enough to photograph three times. This is the first picture. In 1983 I took another photograph from Parker Street. In January 1986 No. 161 was empty and as I thought it might be demolished I photographed the back of these houses from the car park in Parker Street. Later that year No.161 was demolished though No.159 with a large bow window at the back remains.

97 71 SOUTH AUDLEY STREET, MAYFAIR. 30 OCTOBER 1983.
Built in 1744, probably by Edward Shepherd, the house is now an office and has a good interior which I photographed in 1985. Besides this one, there are other fine houses in the street built in the 1730s, though I haven't photographed them yet because of parked cars. In the catalogue from the exhibition *Ciutat Fantasma* (Ghost City), at the Joan Miro Foundation in Barcelona, a writer thought the reason I photograph streets with no cars or people in them is because that is my view of the future of cities – abandoned. This is nonsense. I just didn't like cars in pictures of historic buildings and streets, and as people are usually blurred from the slow shutter speeds I often wait until there are no people in the picture.

98 ARLINGTON STREET, ST. JAMES'S.
4 SEPTEMBER 1982.
This old house probably dates from the 1680s when Arlington Street was built. Many famous people have lived in this street, including Horace Walpole, Charles James Fox, Barbara Castlemaine and Nelson. The white house has been redeveloped since this picture was taken and no longer has the odd door. The name St. James's comes from a leper hospital that stood on the site of St. James's Palace from the twelfth century until 1532, when Henry VIII had the old buildings demolished and built the palace on the site.

99 CABMEN'S SHELTER, NORTHUMBERLAND AVENUE, STRAND.
12 JUNE 1986.

100 CABMEN'S SHELTER, NORTHUMBERLAND AVENUE, STRAND.
1 MAY 1986.
When I heard that this Victorian cab shelter was due to be demolished and replaced with a new shelter (I often buy tea here when photographing in this area) I took two pictures on 1 May, and another of the outside on 12 June, as I didn't like the picture of the outside taken earlier. For the picture of the interior the camera was set up outside the shelter and the exposure was 6 seconds at f/32 with the 155mm lens.

101 CARLTON HOUSE TERRACE, THE MALL, ST. JAMES'S.
21 JUNE 1980.
After the Restoration in 1660 King Charles II had The Mall laid out and opened St. James's Park to the public. Carlton House Terrace was built on the site of Carlton House in 1827-1832 and was designed by John Nash. Carlton House was demolished after King George IV moved from there to Buckingham House.

102 SHOP, RUSSELL STREET, STRAND. 4 APRIL 1980.
You can read anything from this picture according to your political biases. This is a street that leads to Covent Garden. I very much like the whole area as well as this particular image, but as the street was busy when I took this picture, I couldn't get as close to the shop as I wanted. Although I was using my largest lens, the 375mm, there is too much uninteresting detail around the shop. I don't remember if I tried to take a picture from the other side of the street but if I were taking this picture now I would somehow manage to get a closer view.

103 SEVEN STARS, CAREY STREET, HOLBORN. 18 APRIL 1982.
Built in 1602 this pub is across the road from the Royal Courts of Justice and the buildings behind the pub are part of Lincoln's Inn. Dr. Johnson said 'There is nothing which has yet been contrived by man, by which so much happiness is produced as by a good tavern or inn'. Other than churches, most of the old buildings in London are, or have been, pubs.

104 STALLS, COVENT GARDEN.
SUNSET 13 NOVEMBER 1985.
Taken a few minutes after sunset (12 seconds at f/22 with the 155mm lens). This gave good gradation in the sky. There was a fruit and vegetable market here from the middle of the seventeenth century until 1973. The old market buildings, built in 1831-1833 to the design of Charles Fowler in the centre of the square, were renovated and now form a shopping centre and major tourist attraction.